THE SILENCE OF MY WORDS

From Me Through You

JUAN LUIS MBA N.

Index

"You can fly without wings if you have the sky in your head and the wings in your heart."

–Juan Luis Mba Nchama.

A Way

What is "To be"?

A natural way to flow

What's love?

You 2 + your 2 fears = 4 / by your true beings.

Add half of both becoming a full heart.

What's to be mad?

Taking the psycho...path.

What's a tear?

A peace of soul broken as a glass.

But for someone that causes it,just debris.

What's life?

A form of love and hate.

Definitely, you and I.

Who Am I?

Somebody that can fly without wings having the sky in his

head and the wings in his heart.

Who do they think I am?

Somebody that I am certainly not.

What is to live?

It is to right for us,between us,within us.

What's to die?

Silence; light; serenity...peace

Who are you?

Your heart; your conscience; your soul and your being

What should I do with you?

Know that we are one, that you exist because and for

me...therefore respect your life and remember me.

Love Me

Love me like you do, without holding the truth.

Love me how you promised me to and how you decided to;

My eyes are my soul's mirror; although blind, my love for

you could be; I know there is love for me in your soul when

I look through.

Love me as a human being through our lifetime, with honor

in your promise, with the symbol of a ring, as a vivid,

passionate, and unique lover loving me at an extreme. I will

love you as a soldier getting on my knees who will forever

fight for you to bring you peace, even on a battlefield.

Love me with pain; love me with a smile.

Awake that love within me & for me with your touch.

Who am I to decide on top of what my heart wants, and

your love for me has revived?

Love me how you see; love me how I will be.

Love me tender, being expressive, and showing me your

tears, so I can learn from you through your being.

Love me with love; there is no other way; you wouldn't love

me with hate.

Love me with my essence; love me with sense.

Love me as a lover; love me as a friend.

Love me from every inch of your soul because then I'll

know you truly love me for a decision, not for the idea of

being in love caused by the love song you have listened to

every time you were left alone and your heart broke.

Love me, just love me enough, although you can't be

measured and remain unknown.

In how many ways would you be able to love me that could

be considered truth?

If I am in your head and your prayers by God's grace, then

I will suggest you;

Love me like you can, not as I would have told you to.

Love me just like you do.

Loving You

Loving you it is a burning flame of light far from hell.

Where fear it is extinguished, and vanity suffocates.

Loving you it is a place where my spirit can rest; Right on the beating bomb on the left side corner of your chest.

We both know that place, as for them it is known as "a place with no name"

Loving you reminds me that I should be fair; There will be joy, there will be pain, there will be us and not reality in what "they say."

Loving you could be the best of my decisions and the worst of my mistakes.

Loving you it is human, it is flesh but it becomes celestial looking into your eyes and feeling your breath.

Loving you begins with the end game of my bad stands.

Loving you it is being one-being-nature, one heart, one face.

Loving you it is a true story, not a fairytale.

Loving you it is hard, but I will love you harder, because to me it matters.

Don't pretend not loving me; it hurts me, it destroys me and it bothers.

I will surely love you loudly; I will not keep it quiet;

Hopefully, you love as loud or louder.

Love me, but not greater than the father.

Love me enough so that I will know what is he closest thing

to heaven.

In Another Life

In another life, I would have been better; you would have been perfect.

You wouldn't have been neglected; we would have been lovely and not reckless.

We would have been constructive to each other, builders with purposes, not helpless.

We would have been direct, detailed, and positively verbal: selfless.

It would have been our souls speaking, our decisions acting, our forgiveness curing, us being tender fleshless, but we faded away to do it our way.

So, on the way, we could find ways that could lead us to the right way, which, by the way, we're not what we expected anyway.

Therefore, in another life, from the lesson learned in this universe, we should be friends, but that's in another life. I know you, me, and the US...shall we start, continue, or stop?

It's on now, right here, not in another life.

The Players That Got Played

She is window-paining

I am heart-yelling

We are love-fading and compromise-failing

We are both heart-bleeding.

We want to stay thus it is too, we will continue...leaving.

Not the plus but each other;

Not the relationship but as lover

The time has arrived and our time together along with our mind games; It's over

There is no more composure hence a disclosure

We have taken in abundance from each other, we have seen it all and now it is too much exposure.

We once had a good connection; We once had good reception.

We got played by ourselves for ourselves in a place with no name where we found each one's deception.

We once had strong emotions, which is why we failed in the first place.

Love was always a decision that we never made because we thought that if we were two, we could play that game.

I guess next time, we will follow the truth and accept it and not just the bumping organ on the left side of our chest.

The Whimsical

It's capable of sending somebody's heart on fire

That sincerely wants its aims to be desired.

It will twist its masochism with your pain,

your willingness to try with its thirst;

its vision with lies will take its goal with your death.

It wants what it wants, but never what is best for it.

It will angrily hold to its throne, and once able to control

your consciousness, it blocks it.

Its delusion will take you to illusions that are allusions to

the pollution added to your confusion.

Prepare an umbrella for the tears that it will provoke in

your eyes;

for the lack of sleep in your bed;

for the nest of blame in your head;

For your most profound sorrow as your only company

when you cry;

As for the long-lasting pain in your chest that will provoke

you to hate and prevent you from rising.

It is known for being whimsical; "Heart" is how it is

biologically addressed.

It will make you see everything magical.

Its words in your head will sound poetical.

Its songs about love, songs without love, will be classical.

It will sugar code your understanding of the words of the

person it targeted and buy you crystal flowers. It can be

botanical.

Very often, it will make you hysterical.

It will undoubtedly make you cynical.

It will make anything to you as long you're under its

control because it wants what it wants; it's whimsical.

Dress Me Up

I've been naked since yesterday, and you still don't see me.

I have stood soullessly naked, giving you my being.

I have fallen apart and destroyed myself, and instead of you

building me up, your eyes tell me, "Build yourself."

I've been holding back, but I haven't been having you, and

my love contains a lot of love to give, and since you're not

going to take advantage of it, it's not worth having you.

Dress me up so I can restore my skin. Ever since you've

touched it, my soul has become dark.

At this point in life, you continue to have absurd doubts,

concentrating on a possible breakup, While I am the one

insisting on being by your side.

I am still faithful to you; it is not lacking at all sanity

because I love you, out of respect for the bond and duty

because I promised it to you, to your family, and because I

swore it to the highest of all kings.

Dress me up, even if I will no longer see your figure.

Still, you have caused fissures in my heart that have no

plains, that only bleed sadness, loneliness, and bitterness,

alter its texture while hanging is the moon looking at me,

*and there you stand lost, without knowing what you're
going to do.*

*Dress me up because I complied as a friend; I was
prepared for this destiny; your whim was the promise and
the ring, and now that I gave it to you and I'm with you,
you're still doubtful, and I'm still here, alarming myself.*

Dress me, or better, I will.

*At this point, I can't be telling you to "open up" or "tell me"
and not even begging you to "love me".*

We started as friends; we intermediate as lovers

We were war, passion, seduction, damage; we were art.

*An inspired art worked for, struggled instead of drawn, and
painted but unfortunately could not be hung.*

*We were raw souls; we were each other's light when it was
dark.*

*We were chaos and harmony. The highest tower took time
to build, but nothing turned into ruins.*

*I thought I would always dress you, but it is not with my
body you want to be covered with; from what I have seen, it
causes you injuries.*

I took off an expensive garment before your eyes;

Its brand was my blood, made with love, its fabric was my feelings, and its color was my passion for you, but even so, it still means nothing to you.

You could be my queen and I would have become your king, but we stayed as princess and prince, and now you're just someone I loved, someone I dreamed of being able to love.

Now, you're just someone I used to know.

We already know all this, so I'll get dressed.

It was a pleasure to have met you, even though my time was wasted, but I appreciate what I lived through this and to have met you even though I was hurt.

Look now, dress me up; I grant you the separation, I give you freedom advising you that next time you should be concerned about being safe, that you do not make the next person undergo torture, that you avoid hurting we are also people, we are also hearts and souls, besides just be seen as me.

I gave myself up, and you were not entirely sure of yourself. Even knowing that you love me, you will not open up, so if you would excuse me, or you do not, I will get dressed.

I taught you to be naked with your soul, and if until now you haven't done it, maybe I didn't teach you well.

Be that as it may, I'll get dressed, and for the next time, I hope you've organized yourself; until then, hopefully, I won't see you again.

The Ones

If I am still standing before you, I unthinkingly know that you will be behind, backing me up.

If I proceed with our thing, we will move forward despite everything that could harm us and feed what is incorrect.

Even if they throw bullets at me, guarding my back, you are my immunity.

They will tell you I am blind, that I act, and do not think properly.

Isn't that true love?

They see you dry; I have seen you wet in an ocean of tears when crying.

They see you hard; I hug you, so your heart can breathe, and the hardness ends.

They are the same ones who advise you to leave me while I only see your heart.

Since when did a person stop being human due to misinterpretation?

The grandest stage I have seen is where I witness you daily.

Will they tell me that I am also a good actor for that?

They say that for you, I will not be "enough."

If they mean I shouldn't love you enough, they always avoided any life and preferred death.

I want to turn you on so that you give me light and warmth; to learn your pitch and notes as if you were my favorite song and sing you and to you all along; to turn you around so that you can unwrap with my passion; to wrap you in my arms from the moon to the sun.

But I couldn't absolve you if you believed in them, not me.

My "love you" is not false, but rather pleasant because I tell you now, regardless of the result that happens later.

And if you believe them, close your eyes, count to ten, let me go, and I assure you that when you open your eyes, you won't see nor hear of them nor from them.

They are the ones who always speak and do not contribute.

Those who see our relationship grow but abort it.

Those who see us die of jealousy and our love trying to find a passport, so it could die off and fade away.

Those who see us whole even though we are halves and cut us out.

Those who hate that love songs play since they know none, and it hurts them, and they must hurt us too; what do they care?

They add evil, subtract love, and later wonder why they don't have relationships or don't connect.

They comment and do not progress, criticize other people's relationships, poison, and brazenly ask for peace.

Who are they that are known but not seen?

Envy kills and does not cure, an excellent poison for sanity.

If you continue to be so hateful, they will continue to be in the dark.

They are not our relationship; they don't know how it started but plan how it will end.

Now, do we leave ours for some random people we do not know, or do we carry on the total weight of what we carried inside, regardless of what those say?

I have already agreed to the second option; now it's your call.

Stay (With Me)

*I ask your permission to be two flowers planted in the same
place to see you every sunrise.*

*To get up and be the first thing on the surface that I can see
at every sunrise.*

*To emerge from the seed that separates us
To evolve underground within the depths of our being,
grow, and appear.*

*To fulfill a purpose and make a dream come true, please
stay.*

*My stem was straight; you tangled it; I was wild; you
tamed me; I was free; you locked me up, and honestly, I
enjoy that cell; because of it, there is the fruit that I fell in
love with you.*

*Loving You? But how can I not love you? If, in itself, it is
an art.*

Art that you possess and makes you unique in this species.

It's hard for me to study, but I can't stop looking at you.

I love your kisses, but I prefer to kiss you.

*My arms open when greeting you because I want to hug
you.*

I talk non-stop, but I find the art in talking to you.

You are heat, and I am cold; together, we are warm.

The void filled with the brightest darkness, something that never existed.

Give me your warmth, leave your heart with me, stay.

I will stay with you because, after this process, I hope you love me later.

Stay, I don't need to tell you why I insist.

Stay for you, stay for me, wait for us, stay for no end.

This has a solution; there will be an evolution in us.

If I'm on fire, and you're freezing, we create steam

If I'm going and you're calm, let's synchronize

If we feel far from each other, let's connect,

Not in terms of network or sex, but in love for our relationship and with love for God.

If I'm in a storm, and you're in a hurricane, let's avoid it, and when the calm has arrived, let's talk about it.

If I love you, and you love me, we will make peace, recover, create, and love in approval and blessing.

Stay, I want to look into your eyes; in them, I see you through me

I find the answer to what I could have but never had the chance to be in you.

*In you, I remain standing in front of the sea, on the earth,
under the moon and the stars.*

*Allow me to give you a nice ring, most gleaming but
genuine and straightforward, with much more love than
time itself and appreciation than anyone who owns a
platinum one.*

*For the last time, I ask you with all my heart to stay in the
external place and stay with me.*

Stupid in Love

I am excited to have imagined you.

Glad to have found you.

I was enchanted by the fact that we were in love.

I am happy to have shared moments with you and now

internally bled by accepting that you have abandoned me.

I never thought I would apologize for letting my feelings

flow.

I was sorry to feel the most excellent sense in the world and

how sad I am.

I think I'm over it, but these are words of consolation

because I pray to myself, which is wrong, and even though

you have harmed me,

I kneel before God, asking Him to protect you

because you are not only in my thoughts, but I even pray

for you.

My diary keeps letters that, in loving physical form, I had

once given you.

My pen continues to lyrically reproduce the feelings that

until now I feel when thinking of you.

My guitar misses me playing it to sing to you in the

morning.

The grand piano and my fingers can't synchronize; they get

stuck because of your absence.

My heart beats disappointingly slowly, knowing that yours

no longer loves it.

Day turns to night, night to dawn, and I can't sleep.

Your hands were my rattle, your hugs my cradle, and your

voice my lullaby.

The pillow is soft, precious, and peaceful as the moon, but I

don't want his company but yours.

I was hoping you could come back, and I will even omit my

fury

Maybe I was good, but you aimed for something better.

Maybe we sang the love song, but you never got to feel that

love.

I may have acted like your lover, but I was your love

And I find that's the reason why your heart doesn't know

me,

although it has always had my heart

If you took me to the stars, the impact of losing you beat up,

and with them, you took my light because I'm off.

I only know that I am stupid in love.

I don't know whether to blame my illusion or my dreams

Because you're a lovely living nightmare.

You are warm in acting, but in feeling, you are cold

Poor deluded man who is loving you right now; I don't

envy him.

Poor of the one who thinks that, has you.

My condolences to the one who wants you to have.

Players change, but the game stays the same.

I played chess to save my queen.

The board was reduced; that board is my world, and the

end of the game came, and I will remain forever

a stupid in love that lost your end game.

Go and Remain Love that…

You are my heart walking out as a human figure, and my heartbeat felt in another chest, my lips perfectly drawn on yours with its kisses. You're me outside of me. Before we share a bed, I want to tell you this:

I did not buy my love for you; I did not fake it or put makeup on it; instead, it was born from my heart.

Until recently, I did not meet it, but more than convincing me, it captivated me.

I don't know how it started; with spite, I saw it in others; with desperation, I wanted it in my head, and it scares me now that it touched me.

I know that you are unloved, but I love you for good with your wounds, your shame, your insecurities, and your pain.

I want to add that with me, you will not have to defend what is yours

because being yours,

I know who I belong to

and so

If we have just started, let's start by not finishing.

If we just met, let's not stop dating.

If we are here today, it is to unite, not to separate

that if you are afraid, and they turn into nightmares, I will

be part of your dreams.

That you have me in love and that without you by my side, I

can't.

It is usual for you to feel afraid because you feel, but

feelings come and go, and decisions remain; I have decided

to love you because that's how it should be, and that's what

we should want

Shall I undress you or remove the veil?

Do you give me a ring or do I wait?

It all depends on you if it is a no or an "I do."

What Was That We Used To Have?

What did we use to have that's now gone?

Appearance or essence?

Energy or power?

Deep desire or mere interest?

Each other's possessions?

Our individual goods or our well-being?

Hope for an alliance or faith in providing?

What did we use to have that's no longer there?

Hypocrisy or truth?

Coincidence due to age, tastes, interests, or genuine
friendship?

As for our love, did it happen too fast?

Was it because societal pressures burdened us with
responsibilities we couldn't sustain, and we never rose
above?

Did it not matter to us to give or give unevenly?

What did the other bring to the table?

If you didn't give, I didn't reciprocate.

If I looked, you twisted out of fear and ego,
The great irony?

That we were meant for each other... but we only expressed it while looking at the sky, with tears, and on our knees.

Did my voice bring you serenity or anxiety, depending on the tone?

As my beloved, did I nurture you?

Did we know what we were doing, or were we children?

There should have been innocence, mercy, and forgiveness if we were children.

We were adults, irresponsible, fearful, and masochistic in action, not what the heart desires.

We were scared of the heat we generated in each other, perhaps why we ended up so cold.

We found open paths to tempting places, and we left...

We played so much not to lose that we lost everything, not realizing it wasn't a game, and in the end, our bond lost its thread."

Here It Is

Here it is, its material price is 0 figures.

It is natural, fresh, tender, intimate, and innocent, just as it moves and beats.

Here it is; Just as it feels like not existing for someone, it wants someone to live.

It wants to be honest, and it wants to be loved as it thinks it should, but it fails when idealizing everything.

It doesn't want past stories to repeat themselves but hides instead of looking for a light, which sensitizes it.

If you love me, take care of it for me.

It has feelings for you, and I doubt it will resist you.

It sometimes does not know how to express itself, so please be patient.

It is, at all costs, not a conformist.

Please heal the wounds from its past and present so that in the future, with you, it learns to be optimistic.

It needs eloquence, to be harsh with hurtful penalties, and it sure needs decency and be less pessimistic.

It needs more love, care, and healthy intimacy to avoid being publicly rowdy.

It appears upright when it truly seeks to be valued and have someone valuable.

It is jealous, capricious, worried, and often vain. Once you undress it, the confusion and the darkness in it will disappear, and it will get to be seen for what it is: something fearful, affectionate, and kind.

Although the way it often demonstrates it does not help, it is so scandalous.

Yes, it is very dreamy, and its imagination divides it between truth and surreal thoughts, But who didn't discover deep wounds in their being and become argumentative? Who, up to now, due to these wounds, is not an absolutist? Who caused it not to become an extremist? And even having to be divided to be with you, by its erratic nature, will make it want to be the protagonist.

Here is your order as you wanted it.

I wish God gives you patience with it and your strength. God reveals Himself to both of you; maybe He will dress you both.

May He be the one who insists, may He be the one who moves you to a new and only being, for everything old and ugly He purifies and cleans.

As for your order,

It will make you the occasional snub.

It will seem that you pray, fight, and strive in vain.

It appears that it does not want a home that is closer to the
street

Do your duty, do your part, and don't fail.

You will not be precisely the reason; be patient.

If you entrust God this package inside its flesh and that his
soul awaits, the good details will become great, but all love
requires sacrifice, pain, sweat, tears, and blood.

I Did Not Know

Until now, I never indeed considered what was happening to me. I never seriously contemplated it; however, I will admit that I knew something was amiss. It was strange, it was unusual, but not necessarily bad. It was priceless, yet it felt costly, not in a material sense, but more in a way that was neither entirely literal nor figurative.

Up to this day, I can't quite decipher it. Vaguely, I connect it to my senses, but my feelings tend to channel it. Everything was upside down, disorganized, inexplicable, all across the board. Each time it happened, I felt more disoriented. I appeared to be present but needed to be found. Despite always maintaining composure, I seemed disheveled, always well-dressed but falling by its rules, always sweating, stuttering, nervous, and sometimes even hyperventilating.

I thought I was delirious; I thought I wasn't well. I believed I was living too much in my imagination, surrounded by the reality that was unfolding. I considered escaping or avoiding it, pretending to have gone through it. I believed that what was happening was that I was needy. I thought I was inventing movies in my head, that my experiences were like a reel, and my imagination was recording while my subconscious was feeding. I felt suffocated, I was unraveled, I felt powerless, I felt desolate. It was better to stay silent to avoid causing harm or being harmed. I felt ashamed to speak of it; it was embarrassing to express it publicly. I felt uncomfortable and vulnerable every time these thoughts roamed in my head.

I didn't know I had to work through it; I wasn't unaware I had to decipher it. I imagined feeling it someday, but I remain ignorant, knowing that I should confess it one day. How do I do that? But God revealed to me what was happening: all of this was due to a person who unintentionally had caused this whole turmoil.

We unknowingly both arrived at the same conclusion, and with certainty, we knew what we didn't realize was that we were in love.

She Is

She is calling; she's lonely; the painting; she's sorry

She's drawing, trying to float.

She's living, trying to cope.

She's living, losing no hope.

She's a girl, somebody's crush.

She's a woman; she's a soul.

She's a mother, somebody's world.

She's a wife, somebody's love.

She's a sister, somebody's opposite self.

She's a human being, different from the rest.

She's alive; she can fight and cry.

She can learn and can inspire and guide.

She's a conversation; she's my conversation in my intimacy with God.

She is my wife, the best thing I have got.

Writing Your Name

"I want you" is not hard to say.

"I love you" is not difficult to pronounce.

"I have you to the left of my chest" when breathing. That is to say that since I saw you, for you, and to you, I could not resist.

My shadowed eyes do not cover your blue and attractive light.

I don't know how to write your name, but I realized I can only draw it.

I can't have your love; only imagine it.

I don't have your attention; That's why I dream that I'm worthy of it.

I never knew love, but I discover it, feel it, and do it with you. In my dreams, although rather nightmares, when not enjoying having you with me.

You don't wear a cape, but you motivate. You save the life of my love, and for it, you are addicted, even by being flesh and blood and not substance; likewise, you are still a heroine.

I want to drink the coffee color of your eyes at the same time as feeling its warmth.

I want to fall for the beauty of your caffeine, and even if they were black, I would fall hard.

I see men with their women and women with their men.

Here I am:

Waiting for you to look at me, and while I keep the faith that I'll make it, I'm still on the seashore, hesitant, drawing your name under the sun.

What Have You Lost?

-What have you lost?

+My heart

-What can't you find?

+My reasoning.

-What do you think you should do?

+Find it and synchronize it with my being.

-Why do you believe that?

+Because it is worth more than anyone, I have ever given it

to.

-Do you honestly think so? Why?

+Because then I would not be searching for it; instead, I

would be sharing it with somebody else who would

appreciate it, and since that has not been possible up to

now, I will nurture and use it to learn how to love myself.

-Disappointed and busy looking for your other half, I see.

Tell me something tiny seed;

Have you already invested time in the process that growth

requires to flourish? Or have you, at the very least, taken

root underground to emerge on the surface minimally?

See here, tiny seed; You will become a good three. Indeed, you must get rid of the weed you feed on in disbelief that love does not exist, and just then…you will be set free, give good fruits, and be truthful to your being.

I Wish

I hope we learn and apply more than we promise and talk.

I wish we advance more for mental, cultural, spiritual, and personal development than the journey we take when we walk.

I wish we could stop judging, For we are judges out of judgment and with unjust and changing minds.

I wish we could change the vanity of the image for the long-lived beauty of the art of knowing who we are.

I wish they would stop calling us influencers. We are pretty stuck in our lives to flow in any way, contrary to what we portray to the naked eye, and our reality is denied.

I hope we understand that we are not so different, and even though we have various tones of skin, different mindsets, and abilities, we all try to be good, and we all are, indeed, simply people.

I wish you could stop being a live bomb inside your head and start sharing that vibe with reality; I know the world will not put up with you. What's more, it will judge you; however, be you with your life because we are killing ours, and that is why there is so much damage, but I still wish you to live free, fly high, and spread the peace and knowledge you have.

I hope we can learn after seeing this;

So we can stop being strangers who understand each other with gestures but prefer to understand their silence and distance.

I wish we could speak, understand, observe, and analyze.

I wish we could learn to swim and stop drowning.

It's not always them; 90% of the time, it's us inside our heads.

I wish society would allude to its name and could be as natural;

No hypocrisy, appearance, falsehood, envy, and malice.

I am asking a lot, but could that be real? I can only Wish.

What Are You Carrying?

-What are you carrying in your hands?-

+The strength and will make it possible+

-What do you have in your head?-

+The reality that only I can understand

-What do you see through your eyes?-

+The vision of my reality in a foreign world

-What do you have in your heart?-

+ God as my guide, protector, and feeder plus the love

within me+

Along The Way

Along the way, I lived what was given, valued what was taken, and dreamed and cried for what I lived.

Along the way, I was born, now a young adult with a heart looking and feeling like a child.

Being human and emotional does not necessarily mean I was born benign.

I understood that my mouth was a double-edged sword and that I should be careful with what I said.

My hands could soothe and harm the people who attack me and those I love, including myself.

That my hands and mouth could bless and curse others as well.

Along the way, I learned that we can live and not be alive;

That we can still be dead even though our hearts pump blood, and we listen to their beats;

Just as we want to heal wounds, so we hurt ourselves.

Most of the time, we greet by asking, "How are you?" And we answer, "Fine," we fake it.

Along the way, I learned that not everyone who smiles at me is my friend.

Along the way, I learned that friends and enemies are the same person in reverse.

Along the way, I lost and found faith in people.

I think there are people out there who care about others' welfare.

I was curious, conceited, arrogant, and humble along the way.

I remember smiling, cheerful, happy, innocent, and candid.

Despite the anxiety that, society has tried to sink me countless times and give me the chance to become myself.

On the way, they handed me over, I found them, they took me away, and I lost my mind.

Along the way, I learned to say: I'm sorry, thank you, I love you, it hurts, and please.

I learned that acknowledging pain does not make me less of a man and that pain only exists if you let it in.

Along the way, I cried, I smiled, I laughed, I lived, and I died, Not before realizing that "I can fly without wings having the clouds in my head and the wings in my heart."

My Friend

I have given, and you have not returned.

I have waited, but you have never arrived.

I have called, and you have yet to answer me.

I have remained silent; I see that is what you want.

*I've been told about your situation; you haven't
complained.*

*I have listened, studied, and kept quiet; I have not
expressed myself nor given you any advice, and that,
before, was not a problem.*

*Now I see it is bothering me, but you taught me that today's
friendship is what you want to have.*

*At least, that's how you have taught me; I have learned
according to how you have educated me.*

*If now it seems wrong to you, that's how you have
miseducated me.*

*From someone I know to someone I used to see, you've
become.*

*Let's not blame the distance or the proximity; we have gone
too far.*

Don't mention growing up because it's already offensive to be this age and realize that our friendship was never there; that's why it never left.

If I saw you somewhere trust me, I no longer remember, and if so, I don't know where because it was certainly not our place, and you were not my best friend's major backflip, a significant downgrade.

I remember where we were; however, Where are we now, my friend?

Talk to me, and I'll talk to you, but who has been answering in your place? Fear or shame? Uncertainty or Ego? Women? Men? Money? The fact that you did not borrow your shoulder for me to cry on when I ? Or that I am in my moment and know that I do not need you to be around me and I can do great all by myself?

Either way, I forgive you because I love you and due to respect that you were once my friend and thus not my soulmate.

Forgive me, too, because I know that I have not been the good one either, and my silence did not compensate; we are both humans in debt; we were once friends.

Maybe later, we'll be friends for life or just vague memories.

Whether a blessing or a curse, it was a pleasure to have
coincided with you in this life.
God will decide which one will see the other's end.
Side note: we have damaged ourselves, and we both
deserve redemption;
I love you, forgive you, and ask your forgiveness.

I Will Stay

I have waited for you desperately, hoping you would regain hope.

I have seen you take small-giant steps in your dancing wanderings.

I keep following you, although I am not sure I should because you wouldn't want me as a continuous follower.

To me, you are living life outside a home, and every time you die, I will revive you and stay in you as a home.

I will never let you cut your vibrant vibe; instead, let you electrocute other living souls like yours and connect people in a real web.

If it were me, you would be inside,

And for me to be inside, you would do anything

Do not be in the middle, and there is no way, neither side nor remedy

If you flow, you don't get stuck and run away, if you don't get caught inside your liberal prison of thought.

It is you against your ideas, against the pile of your chest, against your senses, against the universe. Your thoughts will make you not feel, and your feelings will make you fall into a prisoner.

You know a lot, but you still have to learn.

By knowing so much, you consume yourself so much that you will turn on, and by the time you get hooked, you will learn that it is not capital, material, or feelings; it is always faith.

While you haven't figured it out yet:

I will stay with you in the darkness and colors.

Within your insipid bitterness, I will give you flavors.

Within your perdition, I will find you.

I will stay with you when you have anxiety.

To remind you that life is not time and human is not age.

When this mundane world wants to change you, when you want to express yourself, and you feel dumb.

Well, you are already a whole world; it will not be, nor will it have half of you.

I will stay to write to you and to help.

Hello, I am you're being what never was.

I have decided to stay with you by faith.

Effort

*If the **grain of sand** you put turns to dust during any difficulty, go ahead and **make an entire desert**.*

*If your tears **have already created a sea**, may they be **sugary** and not salty?*

If, like the star that you are, you don't shine in the place where you are, change your focus because the stars shine in the dark, and if coexistence becomes complex with other celebrities, remember that there is an infinite sky to be part of.

Just because they don't see you don't mean you're not there; just because they see mediocrity doesn't mean there is.

Cause & Effect

When the silence screams, the depth emerges.

When the heart receives so much cold that it gets consumed without anything lovingly, then it becomes an unlovely burden burning.

When the skin is rough on the sensitivity, feelings do not tremble.

When psychology is strong, wisdom puffs up.

When love is absent, loneliness is present.

When the darkness is deep, the light is the one that twists it.

When you write, you think and sigh fluently; the spirit is the one that uses you and evades you from your intelligence, wisdom, and mind.

*Human, delicate, dangerous yet in need, highly superficial, and painfully sunk. Imperfect human, twisted, bewildered, and confused, you are welcome here; you won't just be free, you will **BE.***

It Hurts You

Now it hurts because it bothers you and it doesn't suit you.

It bothers you because it irritates you and is not what you want.

Why are you with words and not with actions?

Why are you always shy and transient to the truth and permanent in what is harmfully hidden and false?

Why comfortable in fluctuation and friction but never in what is beneficial or suitable?

Why should one reach the goal of the union in such a hurry when there is plenty of time and space?

What do people say? What do you feel?

Who are you fighting for? And more importantly, does it belong to you, or does it belong to you?

Are you lost, or do you want to be found?

I know it hurts, but I am less than sorry for you.

You had time to sit, breathe, exhale, and look at the causes and effects from a distance to take advantage, but no.

Your words are shadow and breath; you should stop making excuses; you go crooked and nothing straight.

What will you tell me now if you have neither base nor foundation?

What would you write to me if it's different from the same story? I would have preferred the truth in acts and arguments. You chose to be cowards, quick in your ego, dishonest in terms of fact, and of course, fools!

Now it hurts you, it stings you, it's wounding you, and you should have known that lack of truthfulness encourages ambiguity; whose side are you on?

Not even falseness wants you nearby, and the truth is pain is the only thing that sustains you.

It hurts, but it's your pain; learn the lesson, find consolation, and when you are lost in hell, you will have people to comfort you and take care of your responsibilities; it is no one else or less than the ones you love.

Neither You nor I

In your mind is your movie.

In your mouth is the narrative.

In your body is the act.

In your soul are your essence and feelings.

In your actions, you can contradict or agree with them and become needy.

You see yourself in the dark, eclipsing the truth with your lie, while I see you clearly under the sun because I see you right.

You will say who you think you are; I will tell you who I am.

Which of the two knows themselves inside?

Neither you nor I.

The Problem

Death —human called reproaching it— we are innocents, live our lives to the fullest, our hearts are the ones that fail us, and the feelings they provoke are more vital than us —they justified, intensely— because they dwell within us. Remember that the heart is the first thing created inside our mothers' womb; you can't blame us for this. We start all things just as we begin to live, which is with the heart.

Humans —called the being upon the humans, seriously bothered by their justification and— Are you clumsy because you were born clumsy, or are you clumsy out of fear of righteousness and firmness? —asked rhetorically, annoyed—Don't even bother to answer me.

Yes, the first organ to be created before anything else within you is the heart, so shouldn't it be the first thing you should look at in each of you instead of making judgments based on your "intelligence," instincts, or perception of things? —demanded, indifferently but still disgusted by their presence—

You have many kinds of hearts, but not the appropriate ones. Before you ask me which one you should have with your "smartness" —added sarcastically— I will tell you that it is not the one you have. I will limit myself to that because, as you popularly say in your societies, "you are not ready for this conversation."

You are infinite evil! —answered humans angrily—. Here you are talking about how we have problems; yours is that you are disgusted in your existence, and you have no LOVE!! You take away what is most dear to us regardless of age, medical condition, the meaning of life, or the person in our lives. That's your big problem!

Your foolishness is pathetically funny - Death mocked answered-. I do my job; that's what I was created for. I'm perfect, and I haven't missed any date so far. Did they send you to kill, mutilate, denigrate, and eradicate each other? You are doing the job for meant that I complain —insisted, minimizing the human acts—-. Again, you complain and demand, but you fail. Life and I, even though we are different, respect each other. Do you know any of our disputes during history? Don't answer. Tell me, Men —-demanded furiously— isn't the women given to you to help you in your clumsiness the same one you slander, attack, and harm even when you all come out of one? Do you want to accuse me of destroying lives?

Women! The men to whom you were given to help in their tasks of protecting this world and procreation love them as they are, or do you live on love and romanticization? Don't answer. You have mentioned "Love" well, wasn't it Saint Paul who explained, detailed, and described that:

"Love is understanding; love is helpful and does not envy; love does not boast or get conceited; it is not rude or selfish; it does not get irritated. It does not keep accounts of evil or rejoice at injustice but enjoys the truth. Forgive without limits, believe without limits, wait without limits, endure without limits." Which

of you can tell me that has loved, knows how to love, or is willing to love? Again, you claim you demand but do not deserve it, and I reiterate in your words, "You are not prepared for this conversation.

I, death, am only one step towards heaven or hell, and that is your problem with me, that while I am blunt, you live in a dual nature. Both genders seek a home in the opposite, but you are so stubborn, proud, ignorant, and clumsy to the truth, reality, and yourselves that most of you end up miserable, discouraged, and depressed.

Now, tell me, if everything in the world is old and the only thing that changes is the price of gold, for how much gold have you destroyed the hearts of others and your own for something that already existed but that changed your mind and being?

Men, your body asks you for sex when what you want is love, but you have created such a "macho" society that by wanting to admit what you feel, you are ashamed and make fun of your brothers... now tell me what is worth more: happiness or pride? Your "greatest weakness" and shame are your strength, and when you first accept it... you will be honest, men, not because of biology.

Women, you are eloquent and more versatile, so I do not need to ask you anything - you know what you want, but you live in a glass cage where your idealization and perspective are your prisons, and they always play you. Enriching and constructively beautiful creatures, you are confirmed; your heart is not your curse, but your obsession for control is.

Humans, your history is indifferent to me; I am not the time nor your life; I am death, and although time has not yet come for you, these faults mentioned above of yours already kill you. I only take your souls lately, all your history; you've been the ones to blame for killing your essence.

You constantly complain about your lives - which I'm not complaining about. What's more, it earns me points - and you talk about me with fear.

You disrespect me and your own lives, tempting and provoking me, and by the time I play along, I am the bad guy. If I know anything about you, it is that you are complete when you lose what you want. When I approach a loved one of yours, and I give you time, you value my counterpart, and at the same time, you beg me for more time. You have me, and you respect me. By the time I show up and take them away, I'm the villain, but you never admit what you gain at different levels in your being when I take these people away from you.

Just Sex

He opened his feelings with some verses, but She responded

with a kiss. However, He wanted more of a spiritual

connection, to which She replied:

"Tales are told, sex is touched.

Making love is not born to love, and that's why

sex is my job, my hobby, and my gift."

With a big disappointed and very disillusioned, He

responded:

"Feelings are human; wants could become rights.

Accepting is sacred, loving not only with sex is an

involuntary cause and effect, intoxicating more than the

millions of effects caused by any herbalist and is purer than

the exchange between body and salary."

She replied:

"Sex amuses me, completes me, relaxes me, and does not

give me problems or cause dilemmas.

Love is deluded; it is stupid; it is an illusion.

Humans don't love; if that were the case, the world would

not end, the innocent would not be crying, and the broken

hearts would be respected; there is much of that around.

Sex entertains them, touches them, while love soothes them;

meanwhile, it does not love them."

He responded:

"You don't blame the cause; you learn from it to do well,

know what to want, not to harm, and understand how to

love.

Perfection is not required when you are not perfect.

The weight of others is not projected into other hearts.

You fight, you cry, you suffer, you take time, you choose,

and you live.

Nothing is achieved by pointing fingers; life goes on.

I like the sex I have with you, but I prefer something

complete;

I want your half with the body, feeling without adding

euros, dollars, or pesos."

What He did not want to understand but that ever knew was

that She did not want to chain to untie later.

She did not seek to delude herself with love. She knew that

pleasure made more sense than feeling pain for something

that, in fiction, she had only been able to experience.

She just wanted to sweat, moan, explore, and taste. On the

other hand, He tried to provoke her with a different type of

completion, the hardest of all: the mental healing from her past unhealthy relationships with his love, acts, and affection.

He wanted her, and she wanted a man; he wanted love, but what she had in mind with him was just sex.

We Did It

I thought of her, imagined her, drew her, painted her, and all my life, walking with the misfortune of being alone, I dreamed of being able to have her.

By destiny, by the whim of fate, today we are together; indeed, I never felt so alive.

We did it:

We coincided on this planet, we shook hands, and we still went through potholes, not always with skills, but together, we fled, reaching the primary goal.

We did it, but it didn't start right; I had to fight to feed her heart, listen to her when she needed the pain to liquefy her, put myself in her place, and get out of my comfort zone and get home to put a plate of food on her table.

She has had to deal with many things about me that bother her.

As a couple, we have dealt with people who challenge this relationship, but we discuss everything without fear and with love, sometimes with anger

It was not till offense was over or not showing up that, most of the time, everything was beautiful.

You wouldn't have seen it on social media from me that
stays with me.
We did it; we fell in love like children
We warmed our lonely, wounded hearts
We did, expecting the unexpected, and we stuck with it.
Apart from promising it to each other, we show it.
We compete to see who makes whom happier in a game
that, so far, no one has to lose.
Every day, even if I'm not 100%, it's nice to know that you'll
end it with the person you love; I think so, and whenever
the opportunity presents itself, I'll tell her.
We did it; we argued and hurt each other.
We hated each other and laughed.
We went crazy, and we did it. You wonder what? Love and
war.
So we flow constant balance but are careful not to destroy
ourselves
And if someone does, then we build ourselves.

From Me Through You

I write to you in prose as well as in verse.

I am writing to you because doing it as I do now would tense my body.

I am writing because I have to wait for my feelings and run out of time.

Even though I hate myself for not telling you all this upfront, I promise. I am writing to you.

I am writing to you with my handwriting, that is, by hand, as I give you my heart.

I write to you with letters because many affectionate words would describe what I feel for you, but the summary is called "love."

I am writing to you because a beast has realized that it has found a Belle and beauty itself.

I write to you in a single sentence, but sometimes I end up with countless sonnets.

You may be a muse, which explains your cause and effect.

Sorry, you should not blame me for this. It is your being, your body, and your essence that is part of my universe, in which I write to you with multiple verses every day until I go to bed.

What purpose am I writing this to you for? I am writing to you to remind you that:

If one day you become bitter, I will bring you sweetness with sweets.

If you get dull, I'll lend you and pass on my salt shaker.

I will be your good companion if you are ever surrounded by bad company,

If you feel like a banished princess, I willingly offer to be your knight and, as such, give you all the kingdoms.

If you don't feel loved or unloved, tell me, so I can tell you I love you.

If you see yourself lost, I will gladly be honored to offer you my address.

If you're still lost, don't worry, I'll find you.

It's not fair that you're alone in this.

You don't have to say "I left" because, in me, there will be no "I'm leaving."

Let's do it together, so instead of two "I'm leaving," let it be a "let's go," that will be when love does us part, for now.

Let's enjoy it because

I deeply love the way you love me

as in the past, they did not love me,

and now, neither do they love me nor will they ever love me.

That's why it was always difficult for me to love,

because if I ever had gotten someone who loved me

Today, I would have loved with love

But fortunately, I found you, and I will love you with all my being; because of your teachings, I have already learned to love.

No matter how much or how little, I receive light in your eyes when all of me is in the dark.

As delusional as many could say, you are my reality.

Having a lot or little, I have a soul; who wants vanity?

What you have does not compare to what you give me, my wife.

It is like that, or at least it is for me.

You without me, me without you = an end.

I wish you, you with me = to live.

I am not myself without you, and you are not yourself without me

I identify with you because I see much of myself through you.

Maybe you are my soul mate, I don't know, but be sure: I want you with me until our end.

Could You?

"I hear you say you want to get to know me.

How much of me do you think you can contain to have me?

How much of me can you decipher to read me correctly?

Are you willing to let yourself fall to hold me up?

Will you be able to endure when I stop letting go?

Can you sustain us when I start to fluctuate?

Can you free me when loneliness captures me in my darkness?

Can you illuminate me when my attitude threatens to extinguish me?

Can you find an antidote to withstand and survive my toxicity?

Can you solve the trail of disasters that I bring with me?

Can you be the seamstress who mends and nurtures this disfigured body, this love-starved being, with your thread?

Go ahead, surprise me, do it!

Can a person as obscure as me have a place in your heart?

I'm neutral and getting involved in this matter.

Do you genuinely believe we could be one whole together?

What's your gain?

What makes you think it will be pure?

I don't want you to blame me in the future.

Here, you have a choice; more is needed just to wish, want,

or love.

Tell me, can you?"

I Have Hope

You became the hope that left my heart in yearning; You became the loose cord that unraveled our bond; the tide was turning.

I made a pact with you, an alliance now ending without discerning.

You're the link that's unchained us, our love now burning.

What value in promising but failing to comply,

The audacity to do it while looking into my eyes!

What an insult to my being, how pusillanimous your reply.

What a pity it's to know that I will not be the only one to experience this heartache, but why?

Played by a game not meant for the professional's hand,

Sold, dragged, lost, and suffered for love, as we understand.

You know how to sell yourself; I hope someone will stand,

You know how to play day and night; you've everything planned.

You sweet-talk them, every word calculated, not random,

Breaking the hearts of other men, isn't it like a phantom?

Does it give you wings? What's your ransom?

I'm entirely unfamiliar with the pleasure, but I know the outcome.

Now that you've gained your satisfaction, what's the sensation?

I congratulate you, and you've played your cards with dedication.

Still, I know that you'll fall in love, and have deep contemplation,

I hope that person exists for you, even if it's a fleeting sensation.

Perhaps not the other way around; I know it's your anticipation,

But for a brief moment, they'll bring you joy.

Until they mock you, making you feel lesser, an accusation,

As if, "I can't recall if I saw you," but it's not the same, no consolation.

That's when you'll learn the meaning of love and reciprocation,

That's when you'll begin to respect, think, and care in consideration.

I won't demand that you love me if in yourself there's hesitation,

I hope it will come one day, and I don't wish to see your

desolation.

It's not resentment; sincerely, I wish you more than

salvation,

I hope you let go and shed your layers and your

transformation.

Speak "I love you" inadvertently, without calculation,

Without overthinking it, naturally, that's the proper

inclination.

I hope you fall in love at least once, without hesitation,

Go ahead, woman, embrace the emotion. It's your

destination.

A Men's Apology

We chose the pleasures of your bodies & fully ignored the

riches of your souls.

We forgot how to make love without intercourse

When you, by nature, have been teaching us just that by

being the ones in the flesh to be responsible to bring us to

this world.

Indeed we should have never undermined you, our minds

were under, not you.

Woman, I am sorry and for you I get on my knees;

For as a I am a woman's son you are a woman's daughter,

a woman's peace; a woman's smile and woman's world.

You have helped me to see.

Help me get my nature back and throw what society has

made me to be.

Indeed we deeply need to keep ourselves burning from us

And give birth to the light we are meant to have.

This is a men's apology,not good enough and certainly

uncouscious of what he has;

So was I when you were given to me and you brought a

purpose to my life,today I am in a much profound

sleep,please be by my side and for every pece of your heart

that I have broken in your being, I do sincerely apologize.

Find Me (Underwater)

Find me underwater; Surrounded by my sins, my thoughts, and my deeds.

Find me with shadows shading my life but not my shame; Not wanting to repeat what I did neither find someone to blame;

Instead wanting to be spared from guilt; free from sin; destroyed from my selfishness and be rebuilt.

I know you are here, so please, find me underwater; Being slow in motion; with no function; Full of emotions; Unable to take healthy options; Wishing for a fast-healing potions however, forced to live with wounds that no lotion can avoid its erosion.

Find me underwater;

With no expression…lost into the search of my own foundation; Upside down, in and out, walking, dragging myself to somewhere but with no direction.

Found miserable under my own self-destruction, with no motivation, no soul, no warm-hearted expressions, no love just indecisive confusion…

Lots of questions…0 answers with 100% of them containing 0 solutions.

Find me underwater, with tedious pain in my chest, crooked and hopeless bones, relief me from pain.

Find me in the water, in your holy water, proclaiming your name, take out of the water to holiness.

Take me out of the water, for I need you to do what your name mean, says and does...for it is to save.

Your Thoughts, your space